The WONDERFUL WIZARD OF OZ

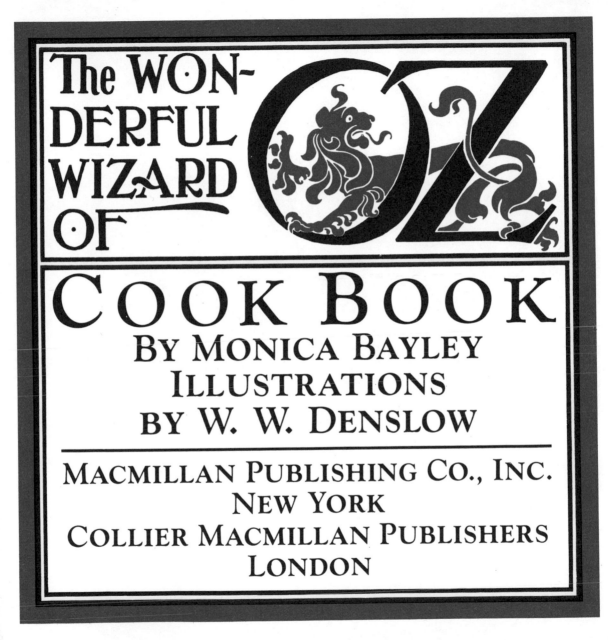

COOK BOOK

BY MONICA BAYLEY
ILLUSTRATIONS
BY W. W. DENSLOW

MACMILLAN PUBLISHING CO., INC.
NEW YORK
COLLIER MACMILLAN PUBLISHERS
LONDON

Text excerpts from L. Frank Baum's **The Wonderful Wizard of Oz**, Geo. M. Hill Co., Chicago, 1900.
Illustrations by W. W. Denslow for L. Frank Baum's **The Wonderful Wizard of Oz**,
Geo. M. Hill Co., Chicago, 1900, and for the poster advertising that book: Courtesy Peter M. Hanff.
Illustrations from original drawings by W. W. Denslow for that book,
pages 9, 29, 57, 81, 89, 101 and 119: Courtesy Prints Division, The New York Public Library;
Astor, Lenox and Tilden Foundations.
Graphic Design by Taylor Nelson.
Composition by Spartan Typographers, San Francisco.

Macmillan Publishing Co., Inc.
866 Third Avenue, New York, N.Y. 10022
Collier Macmillan Canada, Ltd.
Printed in the United States of America

10   9   8   7   6   5   4   3   2   1

Library of Congress Cataloging in Publication Data
Bayley, Monica.
 The wonderful Wizard of Oz cook book.
 Summary: Recipes based on references to food in
"The Wonderful Wizard of Oz."
 1. Cookery—Juvenile literature. [1. Cookery]
I. Denslow, William Wallace, 1856-1915. II. Baum,
Lyman Frank, 1856-1919. Wonderful Wizard of Oz.
III. Title. IV. Title: Wizard of Oz cook book.
TX652.5.B28   641.5'123   81-3708
ISBN 0-02-708530-9   AACR2

CONTENTS

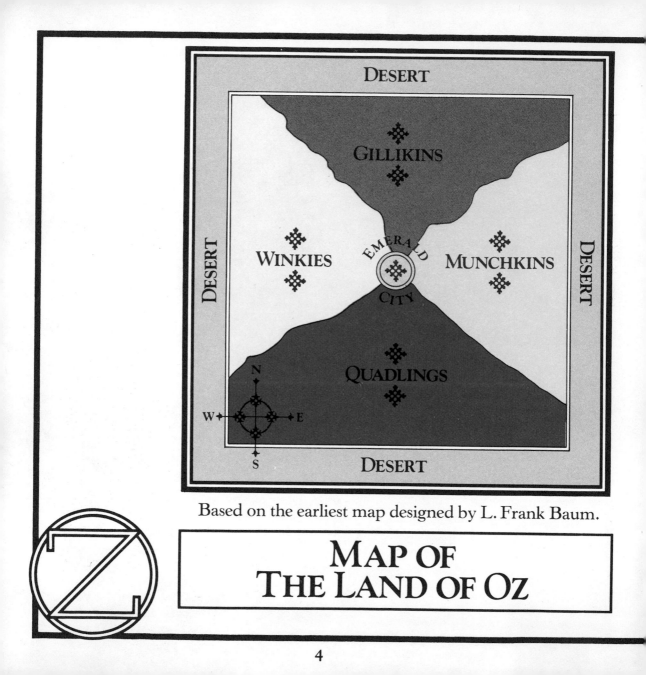

Based on the earliest map designed by L. Frank Baum.

MAP OF
THE LAND OF OZ

4

INTRODUCTION

The recipes in this book are keyed in three ways to Dorothy's adventures in Kansas and the Land of Oz.

First, they are keyed to actual references to food in *The Wonderful Wizard of Oz,* and to the developments in the story. Some dishes are suggested by the introduction of the individual characters as they join Dorothy's entourage and some by the people and things the travelers encounter.

Second, the recipes are keyed to color — an important part of the Oz story. On the Yellow Brick Road and in Winkie Country, yellow ingredients are used. In the Country of the Munchkins, the color is blue; in Quadling Country, red; and in the Emerald City, of course, green.

The third consideration is regional. I associate the Oz "countries" with regions of the United States, and I think the author did, too. Thus the red Quadling country becomes the South — where it's hot; the yellow Winkie Country becomes the West, where the golden sun goes down; and the blue Munchkin country becomes the Northeast, where it's cold. Recipes are appropriate to these regions, with the Midwest represented in the Kansas sections.

This is a cookbook for the young, and for the young in heart — for all who savor the story of Oz.

M.B.

5

AUNT EM'S HELPFUL HINTS

Read recipes carefully. If there are any terms that are unfamiliar, check cooking terms, page 122, before proceeding.

Assemble all ingredients and cooking utensils before starting to cook.

Use standard measuring cups and spoons.

Level spoonfuls of dry ingredients with a table-knife blade.

Preheat the oven to the required temperature.

Rinse things you use as you go along. This makes cleaning up the kitchen at the end easier.

Always ask for help if there is anything that you don't understand.

DOROTHY'S RULES FOR BEGINNERS

Wash your hands before beginning to cook or before handling food.

Wear an apron and tie back your hair if it is long.

Be careful when using electric food machines and appliances. Ask for help from someone who knows how to use them.

Use potholders for handling hot pots and pans, especially when taking them out of the oven.

Be careful when you use sharp knives. Chop or cut on a wooden board and concentrate on what you are doing.

Turn off stove burners before removing pans, and turn off the oven as soon as you have finished using it.

Never leave the stove while heating any type of oil or fat. Watch the pan until the oil is hot, then use it at once.

CYCLONE
COUNTRY

KANSAS
POTATO PANCAKES

3 tablespoons milk
2 eggs, beaten
2 cups peeled, grated raw potatoes
¼ small onion, peeled, minced
2 tablespoons flour
¾ teaspoon salt
¼ teaspoon pepper
¼ teaspoon baking powder

Peel potatoes and soak in cold water for an hour. Drain. Put grated potatoes on dry towel and wring to dry. Combine milk, eggs, potatoes, onion, flour, salt, pepper and baking powder. Beat until thoroughly mixed. Drop by tablespoonfuls onto hot, well-greased griddle or heavy frying pan. Brown on one side, then on the other. Serve hot with applesauce or apple butter. Makes 1 dozen 3-inch cakes.

"Dorothy lived in the midst of the great Kansas prairies, with Uncle Henry, who was a farmer, and Aunt Em, who was the farmer's wife."

SUNDAY BREAKFAST OATMEAL SCONES

1 tablespoon baking powder
½ teaspoon salt
¼ cup sugar
2 cups flour
½ cup quick-cooking oatmeal
½ cup currants
½ cup butter
2 eggs, beaten
½ cup light cream

Sift baking powder, salt, sugar and flour together into mixing bowl. Add oatmeal and currants and stir. Cut butter into small pieces and add. Mix lightly with your fingertips until mixture resembles coarse meal. Mix eggs and cream and stir into dry mixture to form dough. Toss dough onto lightly floured board. (If the dough is too sticky, add a small amount of flour.) Knead gently for a minute. Divide dough into two parts and pat or roll each part into a circle of dough about ½-inch thick. Cut the circles into 8 pie-shaped pieces. Place pieces of dough on greased cookie sheets and bake at 425° for 12 to 15 minutes or until golden. Serve hot with plenty of butter and honey.

AUNT EM'S CHICKEN AND DUMPLINGS

1 (3- to 4-pound) stewing chicken, cut into serving pieces
1 large onion, stuck with 2 whole cloves
1 large carrot, cut in half
2 stalks of celery, cut into 3-inch lengths
2 sprigs of fresh parsley (or 1 teaspoon dried)
3 cups water
2 teaspoons salt
¼ teaspoon pepper
4 tablespoons butter or margarine
3 tablespoons flour
1 cup milk

Dumplings:
1 cup flour
1½ teaspoons baking powder
½ teaspoon salt
2 tablespoons chopped fresh parsley
2 tablespoons shortening
½ cup milk

Put chicken, onion, carrot, celery, parsley, water, salt and pepper into stew pot. Cover and simmer for an hour or more until chicken is just tender. Skim fat off broth and discard. Melt butter in a frying pan. Add flour, stirring constantly.

Add milk slowly while stirring. Cook and stir until smooth and slightly thick. Add to broth and remove from heat.

Make the dumplings: Put flour, baking powder, salt and parsley into a mixing bowl. Add shortening and mix lightly with your fingertips to blend the mixture until it resembles coarse meal. Add milk, stirring with a fork, until well mixed. Bring stew to a boil over medium heat. Turn down heat. Drop dumplings from a tablespoon onto the top of the simmering broth. Cover tightly and cook 12 to 15 minutes. Do not remove cover while steaming dumplings.

TOTO'S ALMOND CHOCOLATE BARK

½ pound butter
1 cup sugar
1 cup chopped almonds
½ pound milk chocolate, melted, or
2 cups milk chocolate chips

Put butter into a small, heavy saucepan and heat until bubbly. Add sugar and stir and boil for about 3 minutes. Add almonds and continue to boil until mixture reaches the hard-ball stage (250°). Remove from fire. Spread on a buttered cookie sheet in a thin layer. When slightly cooled, pour melted chocolate over mixture. Chill in refrigerator. Break into irregular pieces.

UNCLE HENRY'S BEEF SHORT RIBS

6 beef short ribs
(allow one per person; choose lean, meaty ribs)
¼ cup flour
½ teaspoon salt
½ teaspoon pepper
2 tablespoons cooking oil
1 large onion, peeled, cut in half, stuck with 2 cloves
2 to 3 cloves garlic, peeled, minced
1 stalk celery with leaves, cut in pieces
1½ cups beef broth

Pat ribs dry with paper towels. Put flour, salt and pepper into a paper bag. Drop ribs in, 2 at a time, and shake to coat with flour. Put oil into heavy stew pot. Brown ribs in stew pot over moderately high heat. Add onion, garlic, celery and broth. Cover and cook in 325° oven for 1½ hours or until tender.

"Uncle Henry sat upon the door-step and looked anxiously at the sky, which was even grayer than usual. Dorothy stood in the door with Toto in her arms, and looked at the sky too."

DOROTHY'S BROWNIES

2 (1-oz.) squares unsweetened baking chocolate
⅓ cup melted butter
3 eggs, beaten
1½ cups sugar
1 cup sifted flour
¼ teaspoon salt
1 cup chopped walnuts
1 teaspoon vanilla

Melt chocolate in butter over low heat. Beat eggs and sugar together. Sift flour and salt into egg mixture. Add melted butter and chocolate and beat well. Add nuts and vanilla and mix. Put into an oiled 10″ x 14″ pan. Bake at 450° for 12 to 15 minutes. Cut in squares.

"Suddenly Uncle Henry stood up. 'There's a cyclone coming, Em,' he called to his wife. Aunt Em dropped her work and came to the door. One glance told her of the danger close at hand. 'Quick, Dorothy!' she screamed. 'Run for the cellar!'"

WHIRLWIND CAKE

1 cup sugar
⅓ cup butter
2 eggs, beaten
½ cup milk
½ teaspoon vanilla
1¾ cups cake flour
2 teaspoons baking powder
1 teaspoon salt
2 (1-oz.) squares unsweetened chocolate

Put sugar and butter into a mixing bowl and cream with the back of a wooden spoon until mixture is light and fluffy. Combine eggs, milk and vanilla and add to creamed mixture. Beat well. Sift flour, baking powder and salt together and add. Melt chocolate over very low heat. Put about ⅓ of the batter into another bowl, add the melted chocolate and stir until completely blended. Butter a 9" x 9" baking pan. Spoon batters into the pan, alternating light and dark mixtures. Take a a fork and draw the tines through the batter several times to swirl the light and dark mixtures. Bake at 350° for 50 to 60 minutes or until a clean toothpick inserted in the center of the cake comes out clean.

"The house whirled around two or three times and rose slowly through the air."

UPSIDE-DOWN PUDDING

1 dozen dried prunes
1 dozen dried apricots
Water to cover dried fruit
1 tablespoon melted butter
2 tablespoons brown sugar
1 tablespoon lemon juice

Batter:
½ cup sugar
¼ cup shortening
1 egg, beaten
½ teaspoon vanilla
¼ cup milk
1 cup flour
1 teaspoon baking powder
¼ teaspoon salt

Put dried fruit into a saucepan with water to cover and simmer for 20 to 30 minutes until just tender. Drain and put into bottom of deep pie pan, alternating prunes and apricots. Mix melted butter, brown sugar and lemon juice and spread over the fruit.

Cream shortening and sugar. Add vanilla to egg and milk and blend. Sift flour, baking powder and salt together and add these dry ingredients to the creamed mixture alternately with the milk mixture. Bake at 350° for 30 minutes or more until brown on top or until a toothpick inserted in center of pudding comes out clean. Let stand for about 10 minutes.

Loosen edges by running a knife blade around between the pudding and the inside of the pan. Cover the top of the pudding with a plate and invert the pudding so you can serve it fruit side up.

CYCLONE JUMBLES

½ cup butter, softened
½ cup white sugar
½ cup brown sugar
2 eggs
1½ cups flour
¼ cup water
¼ teaspoon salt
½ teaspoon soda
1 teaspoon cinnamon
½ teaspoon cloves
¼ teaspoon ginger
1½ cups walnut meats, coarsely chopped
1 cup raisins
1 cup pitted, chopped dates

Cream butter, sugar and eggs until light. Sift flour, salt, soda, cinnamon, cloves and ginger together and add alternately with water, beating well after each addition. Add nuts, raisins and dates and blend. Drop from a teaspoon onto cookie sheets a few inches apart. Bake at 375° for 10 to 12 minutes until lightly browned. Makes 4 dozen 2-inch cookies.

"In spite of the swaying of the house and the wailing of the wind, Dorothy soon closed her eyes and fell fast asleep."

LAND OF
THE MUNCHKINS

MUNCHKIN FRUIT BOWL

2 pears
2 peaches
2 apricots
½ cantaloupe
½ honeydew melon
1 cup blueberries, washed, hulled
1 tablespoon sugar
1 tablespoon lemon juice
½ cup water

Wash, peel, seed and cut all fruits except blueberries into bite-size pieces. Add blueberries. Sprinkle with sugar, lemon juice and water. Cover and let stand for 15 minutes. Chill and serve.

BLUEBERRIES & CREAM

Blueberries, washed, hulled
Sour cream
Brown sugar

Put blueberries in a shallow bowl. Sprinkle with brown sugar. Spoon sour cream over the berries. Serve in dessert dishes.

"The cyclone had set the house down, very gently — for a cyclone — in the midst of a country of marvelous beauty. There were lovely patches of greensward all about, with stately trees bearing rich and luscious fruits."

BLUEBERRY PANCAKES

1 cup sifted flour
½ teaspoon salt
1 teaspoon baking powder
½ teaspoon soda
2 eggs, beaten
¾ cup buttermilk
2 tablespoons melted butter
1 cup fresh (or frozen) blueberries

Sift flour, salt, baking powder and soda together into mixing bowl.

Combine eggs and buttermilk and stir into dry ingredients until well blended. Add butter and beat until blended. Grease skillet or griddle lightly before first cakes are baked and between bakings. To test the griddle for readiness to bake, drop a few drops of water on it. If the water bounces and sputters instead of boiling away, the griddle is hot enough. Drop the batter from a mixing spoon onto the griddle. Make cakes about 4 inches wide. Drop 5 or 6 washed, stemmed blueberries on top of each cake. Bake until small bubbles appear. Turn and bake until lightly browned on second side. Serve with plenty of butter or maple syrup.

SPOOKY SPONGE CANDY

1 cup sugar
1 cup dark corn syrup
1 tablespoon white vinegar
1 tablespoon baking soda

Put sugar, corn syrup and vinegar in deep saucepan. Bring to a boil and cook, stirring constantly, until sugar is dissolved. Scrape crystals that cling to the sides of the pan down into the mixture, insert candy thermometer and cook without stirring until the thermometer reaches the hard-crack stage (300°) or when a few drops of the hot syrup dropped into cold water separate into brittle threads. Remove from heat. Stir in baking soda. Pour into a shallow buttered pan (8″ square is a good size). Watch the mixture turn into candy sponge. Cool and break into chunks. Wrap chunks in foil or waxed paper.

"The little old woman walked up to Dorothy, made a low bow and said, in a sweet voice, 'You are welcome, most noble Sorceress, to the land of the Munchkins. We are so grateful to you for having killed the wicked Witch of the East, and for setting our people free from bondage.'"

BEWITCHING KISSES

3 egg whites
½ teaspoon baking powder
⅛ teaspoon salt
1 teaspoon vanilla
1 teaspoon vinegar
1 teaspoon water
1 cup sifted sugar
½ cup ground almonds

The secret to making good meringue kisses is that you must beat the egg whites until they are stiff, add the sugar slowly and bake the kisses in a slow oven.

Put egg whites, baking powder and salt into a mixing bowl and beat until foamy. Combine the vanilla, vinegar and water and add. Beat until stiff. Add sugar slowly, a tablespoonful at a time, beating as you add. Add ground almonds. Drop mixture from a tablespoon onto lightly greased cookie sheet. Bake at 250° for 40 minutes or more until kisses will hold their shape but are not too dry. (They should be slightly chewy in the middle.)

"She came close to Dorothy and kissed her gently on the forehead. 'I will give you my kiss, and no one will dare injure a person who has been kissed by the Good Witch of the North,' she said."

MAGIC LEMON PUDDING

¾ cup sugar
3 tablespoons flour
1 cup milk
3 egg yolks, beaten
Juice of 2 lemons and grated peel
3 egg whites, beaten stiff

Mix in order given. Place in greased pudding dish. Set dish in pan of hot water. Bake at 325° for 45 minutes. The custard will settle on the bottom and the sponge cake will rise to the top. It's magic!

MUNCHKIN FRUITS & NUTS

Seedless grapes
Green and yellow melons, peeled and cut into
bite-size cubes
Peaches, apricots, pears and apples, peeled, pitted
and seeded, cut into slices
Orange and grapefruit, peeled, membrane removed
from sections
Strawberries, raspberries and blueberries
Bowls of pecan and walnut meats

Put prepared fruits into a bowl, sprinkling each layer of fruit with powdered sugar as you fill the bowl. For each quart of fruit pour over ¼ cup lime or lemon juice. Stir lightly. Let stand for an hour. Chill. Serve with bowls of nuts.

"Five little fiddlers played as loudly as possible and the people were laughing and singing, while a big table nearby was loaded with delicious fruits and nuts, pies and cakes, and many other good things to eat."

MUNCHKIN CURRANT BREAD

1 cup milk

1 heaping tablespoon shortening

1 cup cold water

1 package dry yeast dissolved in ¼ cup lukewarm water

1 tablespoon salt

1 tablespoon sugar

4 cups unbleached flour

½ cup unbleached flour for kneading

1 cup currants, floured

Put milk into a saucepan and bring to scalding point. Remove from heat. Add shortening and stir until it melts. Add cold water. Let cool until lukewarm, then add softened yeast, salt and sugar and stir until dissolved. Transfer to large, deep mixing bowl. Add flour about 1 cup at a time, beating well after each addition until you can't stir the dough. Add currants. Sprinkle flour on the kneading board or counter, flour your hands and toss the ball of dough onto the board. Flatten the dough and knead it by folding it over and pressing it down with the heels of your hands. Turn it around on the board as you knead and keep folding and pressing it down for about 5 minutes until the dough is smooth and elastic. Put the kneaded dough back in the mixing bowl, cover with a clean cloth and set in a warm place to rise for about 1½ hours or until it doubles in bulk. After it doubles put it back on the floured board, punch it down and divide it in half.

Form into 2 loaves. Put into 2 greased regular-size (4½" x 8½") bread pans. Cover with cloth and put in warm place to rise for another ½ hour. Preheat oven to 375°. Bake for 50 to 60 minutes until loaves are golden brown. Remove from oven.

Take a knife blade and run it around the insides of the pans to loosen the loaves. Carefully remove loaves from pans and let them cool on a wire rack.

BLUE PLUM COMPOTE

1 cup sugar
2 cups water
Pinch of salt
6 thin slices of lemon
4 cups prepared fruit: 2 cups blue plums, washed
4 apricots, peeled
3 small peaches, peeled

Combine sugar, water, salt and lemon slices in deep saucepan. Bring to a boil and simmer for a minute or two. Drop plums into poaching syrup and simmer gently until barely tender. Remove with slotted spoon and set aside. Repeat this poaching process with apricots and peaches. Remove syrup from heat and let cool a bit. Put fruit back into syrup and let cool in the liquid.

"The houses of the Munchkins were odd-looking dwellings, for each was round, with a big dome for a roof. All were painted blue, for in this country of the East blue was the favorite color."

BOQ'S HOT POT

2- to 3-pound pork loin
1 smoked ham hock or half of a smoked pork butt
½ pound thick-cut bacon
3 pounds sauerkraut
2 cloves garlic
½ teaspoon pepper
Few sprigs of fresh dill or ½ teaspoon dill weed
Water to cover
2 garlic sausages
6 medium potatoes
4 knockwurst or large frankfurters

Line the bottom of a Dutch oven with bacon strips. Put sauerkraut into a large bowl and cover with cold water. Rinse it well and then remove it one handful at a time, squeezing the sauerkraut hard to extract all the water. Put pork loin and ham hock into the bottom of the pot. Put sauerkraut all around the meat. Add garlic, pepper and dill. Add water to cover. Cover and put into a 325° oven for 4 hours. Add garlic sausages the last half hour and the knockwurst the last quarter of an hour. During the last half hour, scrub the potatoes and boil them with the skins on until they are tender. When the hot pot is ready to serve, put meats in the center of a platter, arrange the rest of the ingredients around the meats, including the hot potatoes, and serve. Serves 6.

CORN-SAUSAGE CASSEROLE

1 pound ground pork sausage
1 can (16-oz.) cream-style corn
3 cups cooked noodles

Sauté crumbled sausage in frying pan until brown. Drain. Put into buttered baking dish. Add noodles and corn and mix. Bake uncovered at 325° for 25 minutes.

"Dorothy ate a hearty supper and was waited upon by the rich Munchkin himself, whose name was Boq. She watched a wee Munchkin baby, who played with Toto and pulled his tail and crowed and laughed in a way that greatly amused Dorothy. Toto was a fine curiosity to all the people, for they had never seen a dog before."

33

BREAD FOR TRAVELERS

2 cakes compressed yeast or 2 packages dry yeast
½ cup lukewarm water
2 cups lukewarm milk
1 teaspoon salt
¼ cup vegetable oil
4 tablespoons molasses
1 cup unbleached flour
4 cups whole-wheat flour
½ cup unbleached flour for kneading

Dissolve yeast in lukewarm water in small bowl or cup and stir after it softens. Put lukewarm milk into large mixing bowl. Add salt, vegetable oil and molasses and stir well. Add yeast. Add unbleached flour and whole-wheat flour a cup at a time and stir well after each addition. Turn dough out onto a floured board and knead for 5 minutes. The dough will be a bit sticky. Put it back into the bowl, cover it with a thin, clean cloth and set it in a warm place for an hour or until it rises and is double in bulk. Punch it down, cut dough in half and form 2 loaves. Put into well-greased bread tins, cover with cloth and let rise in warm place until double in bulk. Bake in preheated 375° oven for 50 minutes. Loosen around edges of loaves and remove from pans. Cool on a rack.

"She took a little basket and filled it with bread from the cupboard."

ROCKY ROAD CANDY

2 cups milk-chocolate chips
3 cups miniature marshmallows or
regular size marshmallows cut into bits
1 cup chopped walnut meats

Melt chocolate chips in top of double boiler. Grease an 8-inch-square pan. Put marshmallows and nuts into pan. Pour melted chocolate over them and stir gently until mixed. Chill until firm. Cut into cubes. Makes 3 dozen 1-inch cubes.

"'The country here is rich and pleasant, but you must pass through rough and dangerous places before you reach the end of your journey,' said Boq. This worried Dorothy, but she knew that only the great Oz could help her get back to Kansas again, so she bravely resolved not to turn back."

YELLOW BRICK ROAD

Yellow Brick Corn Bread

1 cup cornmeal
½ cup flour
2 tablespoons sugar
1 teaspoon salt
3 teaspoons baking powder
1 egg, beaten
1½ cups milk
2 tablespoons butter, melted

Combine cornmeal, flour, sugar, salt and baking powder and sift together into a mixing bowl. Combine egg and milk and stir into dry mixture. Add butter. Beat until blended. Turn out into a buttered 9″ x 9″ baking pan. Bake at 375° for about 25 minutes or until golden brown. Cut into brick-shaped pieces and serve hot with plenty of butter.

BACON AND CHEESE BRICKS

Slices of rye bread (allow at least 2 per person)
6 slices raw, lean bacon
½ pound Cheddar cheese
½ onion, peeled, chopped
3 teaspoons prepared mustard

Trim crusts and enough bread from slices to shape the slices into rectangles. Put all the rest of the ingredients through a meat grinder and mix well or process in food processor until of spreading consistency. Spread on the bread slices. Place on a cookie sheet and broil until brown and bubbly.

RED ONION & BACON SANDWICHES

8 slices of bread
Mayonnaise
4 wafer-thin slices of red onion
4 thin, crisply-fried slices of bacon
¼ cup minced parsley

Spread 4 slices of bread with mayonnaise. Arrange 1 slice of red onion on each piece of bread, top with 1 slice of bacon, and sprinkle with parsley. Spread the other 4 slices of bread with mayonnaise and put on top. Cut into halves.

QUICK & EASY CORN SAUTÉ

6 wieners
1 can cream-style corn
1 green pepper, seeded, chopped
3 green onions, chopped
2 tablespoons oil for frying

Drop wieners into boiling water. Simmer for about 5 minutes. Drain and let cool a bit. Cut into ½-inch-thick slices. Sauté onions and pepper in oil for a few minutes. Add wieners and sauté for another few minutes. Add corn and simmer, stirring often, for about 5 minutes. Serve on crisp pieces of toast.

"When she had gone several miles she thought she would stop to rest, and so climbed to the top of the fence beside the road. There was a great cornfield beyond the fence, and not far away she saw a Scarecrow, placed high on a pole to keep the birds from the ripe corn."

ROADSIDE PICNIC EGGS

4 eggs, at room temperature
¼ teaspoon salt
½ teaspoon dry mustard
¼ teaspoon pepper
1 teaspoon vinegar
1 tablespoon mayonnaise
2 tablespoons minced, cooked ham

Fill a pan with water to cover eggs. Bring water to a boil. Put eggs into water gently, using a slotted spoon. Turn heat down until water barely simmers and cook eggs for 20 minutes. Lift eggs out of pan with slotted spoon and put into bowl of ice water to cool. When eggs are cold, remove shells and cut each egg in two lengthwise. Scoop out yolks and set whites aside. Combine rest of ingredients with yolks in a shallow bowl and mix and mash with a fork until well blended. Make 8 balls about half the size of an egg yolk and put one in each white. Smooth down with a knife blade.

"The Scarecrow found a tree full of nuts and filled Dorothy's basket with them, so that she would not be hungry for a long time."

SCARECROW SURVIVAL SNACKS

2 cups mixed nuts, broken into small pieces
½ cup coconut flakes
1 cup shelled sunflower seeds
1 cup dried fruit bits (prunes and apricots)
½ cup raisins

Mix all ingredients together and store in tightly covered glass jar. Package small amounts in plastic sandwich bags to tuck into your pocket.

PEANUT BUTTER TOAST

Slices of toast (2 per sandwich)
Slices of bacon (2 per sandwich)
Peanut Butter
Mayonnaise

Fry bacon slices until crisp. Remove from pan and drain on paper towels. Chop into bits. Spread one slice of toast with peanut butter and top with bacon bits. Spread second slice of toast with mayonnaise and put slices together.

HAYSTACK SANDWICHES

1 can shoestring potatoes
4 slices of Cheddar cheese
4 slices of tomato
4 slices of onion
4 slices of bacon
Sweet pickle relish for topping

Arrange 4 small (6″ diameter) foil pans on a cookie sheet. Make a layer of shoestring potatoes in each pan. Top with slices of cheese, tomato and onion in that order. Cut bacon slices in half and put two pieces on each sandwich. Broil until bacon is crisp. Top each stack with a spoonful of relish. Makes 4 sandwiches.

SCARECROW SANDWICHES

For 4 open-face sandwiches:
2 whole-grain English muffins or whole-wheat buns
4 slices of Cheddar cheese
4 tomato wedges
4 ripe olives, pitted, cut in halves
4 carrot tips

Split muffins or buns in half. Cover each half with a slice of cheese. Make a mouth with a tomato wedge, eyes with the olive halves, and a nose with a carrot tip. Put under the broiler just long enough to melt the cheese.

OLD-FASHIONED ICEBOX COOKIES

½ cup brown sugar
½ cup white sugar
¾ cup butter, softened
1 egg, beaten
1½ cups flour
1½ teaspoons baking powder
¾ cup minced walnuts
1 teaspoon vanilla

Cream sugars and butter until light. Add egg and beat. Sift flour and baking powder together and add to creamed mixture. Add walnuts and vanilla and mix to form soft dough. Shape into a roll about 3 inches in diameter. Wrap in waxed paper and chill in refrigerator overnight or put into freezer for ½ hour until firm. Cut into ¼″ slices. Put slices on greased cookie sheets and bake at 400° for 6 minutes or until just golden. Cool. Makes 4 dozen cookies.

" 'Well,' said Dorothy, 'let us go.' And she handed the basket to the Scarecrow. Toward evening they came to a great forest where the trees grew so big and close together that their branches met over the road of yellow brick."

WOODCHOPPER'S BEEF

1 tablespoon butter
½ cup chopped onion
1 pound lean, ground beef
½ teaspoon salt
⅛ teaspoon pepper
⅛ teaspoon thyme
1 egg
1 tablespoon catsup
2 tablespoons oil for frying

Put butter into a frying pan. Add onions and fry until tender over low heat. Remove onions from pan and put into a mixing bowl. Add all the rest of the ingredients and beat and mix with a spoon until blended. Divide mixture into 4 parts and shape each part into a ¾-inch-thick patty. Heat oil until hot and fry patties for 3 minutes on each side. Serves 4.

"One of the big trees had been partly chopped through, and standing beside it, with an uplifted ax in his hands, was a man made entirely of tin. He stood perfectly motionless, as if he could not stir at all."

TIN WOODMAN CHIPS

6 medium baking potatoes
Oil for deep frying
Seasoned salt

Scrub baking potatoes and slice very thin. You need not peel them. Put slices in cold water to cover and let stand for 2 hours or more. (Change the water several times while the potatoes are soaking.) Drain and pat dry with paper towels. Heat oil to deep-fry temperature (375° to 400°) and fry slices, about a cupful at a time, until golden. Stir slices as they fry to keep them from sticking to each other. Remove with slotted spoon and drain on paper towels. Sprinkle with seasoned salt.

"The Tin Woodman gave a sigh of satisfaction and lowered his axe. 'This is a great comfort,' he said. 'I have been holding that axe in the air ever since I rusted, and I'm glad to be able to put it down at last.'"

TIN WOODMAN
NUTS & BOLTS

½ pound shelled salted peanuts
½ pound mixed nuts
3 cups bite-size shredded wheat biscuits
5 cups round oat cereal
1½ teaspoons seasoned salt
4 cups rice cereal
3 cups thin pretzels, broken in half
1 cup melted butter or ½ cup butter & ½ cup margarine
1½ teaspoons Worcestershire sauce
1½ teaspoons garlic salt

Put all ingredients into a large roasting pan and mix thoroughly. Roast in a 250° oven for 1½ to 2 hours, stirring often with wooden spoon. Makes a gallon. Can be stored in tightly sealed jars for a couple of weeks.

TINNED CORNED BEEF HASH WITH DILL

2 (15-oz.) cans corned beef hash
3 tablespoons cooking oil
1½ cups mixed raw, chopped vegetables — onions, carrots,
celery, kohlrabi, green pepper (make your own mixture)
1 teaspoon dill weed
Salt and pepper to taste

Heat oil in large, heavy frying pan. Sauté onions and green pepper briefly, then spread hash in an even layer in pan. Add rest of vegetables. Sprinkle with dill weed. Cook over medium heat until brown crust forms on bottom. Turn hash over in sections with a spatula and brown the other side. Repeat this process a couple more times until vegetables are just barely cooked.

"It was a bit of good luck to have their new comrade join the party, for soon after they had begun their journey again they came to a place where the trees and branches grew so thick over the road that the travellers could not pass."

Cowardly Lion Quivering Gelatin

½ cup cold water
2 tablespoons unflavored gelatin
½ cup boiling water
½ cup sugar
1 cup ice water
1¾ cups orange juice
4 tablespoons lime or lemon juice
1 tablespoon grated orange peel

Soak gelatin in cold water until soft. Heat ½ cup water to boiling in a saucepan. Add gelatin and stir until gelatin is dissolved. Add sugar and stir until sugar is dissolved. Remove from heat. Add ice water, orange and lime juice and stir well. Add grated orange peel. Pour into a buttered quart-size mold. Chill until quivery.

" 'You are nothing but a big coward', Dorothy said. 'I know it', said the Lion, hanging his head in shame. 'I've always known it'."

CHEESECAKE FOR THE QUEEN

Crust:
1 package (6-oz.) zwieback
½ cup melted butter
¼ cup sugar
½ cup currants, washed and dried

Filling:
1 pound baker's dry cottage cheese
3 eggs, separated
½ cup sugar
¼ cup lemon juice
1 tablespoon grated lemon peel
¼ teaspoon salt
1 cup heavy cream

Grind the zwieback or crush fine. Stir in sugar and melted butter. Reserve ½ cup of mixture for top. Butter a 12-inch springform pan. Pat and press the crumb mixture with the back of a spoon to form a crumb crust on the bottom and sides of the pan. Chill thoroughly.

Put the cheese through a sieve and set aside. Beat egg yolks until light, then add sugar and beat again. Add lemon juice and blend. Stir in cheese, grated lemon peel and salt. Whip the cream and fold in. Beat egg whites until stiff and fold in.

Pour batter into the pan. Sprinkle currants on top. Sprinkle reserved crumb mixture on top. Bake at 250° for 1 hour. Turn off heat and leave cake in the oven with the oven door ajar for another hour. Chill. Serves 10.

FIELD MOUSE NIBBLES

¼ pound butter
¼ pound sharp Cheddar cheese, grated
1 cup flour
½ teaspoon cayenne pepper
¼ teaspoon salt

Mix all ingredients until smooth. Chill for ½ hour. Shape into small balls (½-inch). Place on a cookie sheet. Flatten balls slightly with fork tines. Bake at 350° for 10 minutes or until lightly browned.

" 'Only a mouse!' cried the little animal, indignantly, 'why, I am a Queen — the Queen of all the field mice!' "

HOT CHEESE SANDWICHES

¼ pound Cheddar cheese
¼ pound mozzarella cheese
½ pound ground ham
½ bell pepper, washed, seeded
1 medium onion, peeled
Slices of bread

Cut ingredients into chunks or cubes and put through a meat grinder using a coarse disc. Mix well and spread on slices of bread. Bake in 350° oven until toasted and bubbly.

"They came from all directions, and there were thousands of them: big mice and little mice and middle-sized mice; and each one brought a piece of string in his mouth. It was about this time that Dorothy woke from her long sleep and opened her eyes. She was greatly astonished to find herself lying upon the grass, with thousands of mice standing around and looking at her timidly."

Imperial Rice Pudding

1 quart milk
½ cup long-grain rice
½ teaspoon salt
5 tablespoons sugar
Pinch each of nutmeg, cinnamon and ground ginger
2 egg yolks, beaten with 2 tablespoons cold water
1 teaspoon vanilla
Ground cinnamon for topping

Put milk, rice, salt, sugar and spices into deep, heavy pot and cook, covered, over low heat for 2 hours until mixture thickens. Stir about every 15 minutes. Remove from fire, stir in egg yolk mixture and vanilla. Return to fire and cook over low heat for a few more minutes. Serve warm with ground cinnamon sprinkled on top.

"The woman now called to them that supper was ready, so they gathered around the table and Dorothy ate some delicious porridge and a dish of scrambled eggs and a plate of nice white bread, and enjoyed her meal."

DELICIOUS PORRIDGE

2 cups water
1 cup rolled oats
¼ teaspoon salt
Brown sugar

Put water into a heavy saucepan and bring to a boil. Add salt. Sprinkle oats onto the boiling water slowly, while stirring. Stir and cook for about a minute, then turn down heat, cover pan and let mixture cook gently for about 15 minutes or until the water is absorbed. Sprinkle with brown sugar and serve with cream. Serves 4.

SCRAMBLED EGGS

4 eggs
2 tablespoons butter or margarine
Salt and pepper to taste
¼ cup minced parsley

Crack shells and drop eggs into a mixing bowl. Beat with a fork or wire whip for about half a minute. Heat butter in large skillet over medium heat. When butter bubbles and coats bottom of pan, pour beaten eggs into pan. Cook for half a minute. Take a spatula and stir eggs gently to allow raw parts of mixture to run to the bottom. Turn any uncooked parts over gently and cook until eggs are completely cooked and light and fluffy. Add salt and pepper to taste. Sprinkle parsley on top.

A LOAF OF
NICE WHITE BREAD

1 cup lukewarm water
1 cake compressed yeast (⅔ oz.) or 1 package dry yeast
1½ teaspoons salt
2 teaspoons sugar
2 tablespoons melted shortening
3 cups sifted flour
Melted shortening for brushing top
Cornmeal for sprinkling cookie sheet

Put the water into a large mixing bowl. Add crumbled compressed yeast or dry yeast and stir until dissolved. Add salt, sugar and shortening. Add flour and stir to make dough. Turn dough out onto a lightly-floured board and knead until the dough is elastic and smooth. Put into a greased bowl, brush the top with melted shortening, cover with a clean cloth and put in a warm place to let dough rise until it doubles in bulk. Punch down and let rise again until double in bulk. Punch down, form into a long, narrow loaf. Roll the dough gently back and forth to lengthen the loaf and taper ends until the loaf is the right length for a cookie sheet. Place diagonally on a greased cookie sheet that has been sprinkled with corn meal. Make slashes crosswise at 2-inch intervals on top of the loaf. Brush with cold water. Let rise uncovered until double in bulk. Bake in 375° oven for 30 minutes or until light brown and firm.

FARM DOUGHNUTS

3 eggs, beaten
1¼ cups sugar
¼ cup butter, melted
1 cup buttermilk
4 cups flour (approximately)
2 teaspoons baking powder
1 teaspoon soda
½ teaspoon salt
½ teaspoon grated nutmeg
Oil for deep frying

Add sugar to eggs and beat well. Add butter. Stir in buttermilk. Sift flour, baking powder, soda, salt and nutmeg together and add to egg mixture to form dough. Chill dough for at least an hour. Roll out on lightly floured board to about ½-inch thickness. Cut with doughnut cutter. Fry in deep fat at 375°.

(Use a heavy, flat-bottomed pan deep enough so that you have it only half-filled with oil and have plenty of room to move the doughnuts around. Use a pancake turner to slide them into pot and a slotted spoon to remove them when they are brown. Dip the pancake turner into the hot fat before picking the doughnut up. Turn each doughnut as soon as it is brown on one side. Fry only a few at a time and let the oil come back up to temperature between fryings. Drain on paper towels. When doughnuts are cool, sprinkle them with sugar.)

Hot Chocolate

6 tablespoons cocoa
4 tablespoons sugar
⅛ teaspoon salt
½ cup water
3 cups milk
Marshmallows for topping

Put cocoa, sugar and salt in the top of a double boiler and stir until blended. Add water. Bring to a boil and stir, over direct heat, for 2 minutes. Place over simmering water in bottom of double boiler. Add milk. Stir and heat until hot. Cover and let stand over hot water for 5 minutes. Beat with rotary beater or whisk just before serving. Top each serving with a marshmallow.

THE
WONDERFUL
EMERALD CITY
OF OZ

SPARKLING LIMEADE SODA

Limes
Sugar
Soda water
Lemon sherbet

For each cup of soda water, add 1½ tablespoons lime juice and 3 to 4 teaspoons sugar. Put soda water, lime juice and sugar into a soda glass and stir until sugar is dissolved. Add 1 scoop of sherbet.

FRESH MINT ICED TEA

¾ cup black tea leaves
Small handful of fresh mint leaves
3 quarts of boiling water
Juice of 1 lemon and 1 orange
Sugar to taste

Put tea leaves and mint leaves in large saucepan with lid. Pour boiling water on leaves. Cover and let stand for 3 minutes, then strain. Cool a bit. Add fruit juices and sugar to taste. Pour into 3 quart-size glass jars and chill. When ready to serve, put a few ice cubes in each jar and shake until tea is foamy on top. Serve in tall glasses with sprig of mint on top.

GATEKEEPER'S CHEESE LOG

½ pound shredded sharp Cheddar cheese (2 cups)
⅓ cup crumbled Roquefort Cheese
1 garlic clove, finely minced
½ cup sour cream
¼ teaspoon Tabasco sauce
1 teaspoon Worcestershire sauce
1 teaspoon white pepper
½ cup finely minced parsley

Put Cheddar and Roquefort cheeses in a mixing bowl. Mix garlic, cream, Tabasco sauce, Worcestershire sauce and pepper together. Add to cheese and mix until well blended. (You can blend it with your fingertips.) Form into a roll about 2 or 3 inches in diameter. Spread minced parsley on piece of waxed paper. Roll cheese log in parsley to coat entire surface. Chill. When ready to serve, take log out of refrigerator and let it stand to room temperature. Cut into thin slices to put on toast or crackers.

"As they walked on, the green glow became brighter and brighter. In front of them, and at the end of the road of yellow brick, was a big gate, all studded with emeralds that glittered so in the sun that even the painted eyes of the Scarecrow were dazzled by their brilliancy."

GREEN SPLIT PEA SOUP

1 pound green split peas
3 stalks celery, chopped
1 large onion, peeled, minced
2 potatoes, peeled, sliced thin
3 carrots, scraped, chopped
1 large smoked ham shank
Salt and pepper to taste

Soak peas overnight in 3 quarts of water. Drain in morning.
Put into deep soup pot and add 3 quarts of boiling water,
vegetables and ham. Bring to a boil, turn down heat and simmer for 3 hours, stirring occasionally during last hour to
keep from sticking. Remove ham and cut off meat, discard-
ing bones. Cut ham in small pieces and put back in pot.
Season to taste. (Put through a food mill if you want it to be
completely smooth.) Add 2 cups of half-and-half if you want
to make it creamier. This soup will thicken if you store it in
the refrigerator, so stir it well before you reheat it.

SPINACH SALAD

1 pound spinach, washed, dried, stemmed
4 slices bacon
2 teaspoons sugar
3 tablespoons vinegar
¼ teaspoon salt
¼ teaspoon pepper
6 scallions, chopped, or ½ small red onion, grated

Fry bacon until crisp. Remove from pan, drain on paper towels, crumble. Combine sugar, vinegar, salt and pepper. Pour into warm bacon fat, stirring fast. Cut spinach leaves into bite-size pieces and put into salad bowl. Add chopped onions and crumbled bacon. Pour warm sauce over salad and toss. Serve hot.

69

STUFFED GREEN PEPPERS

4 green bell peppers
2 tablespoons oil
3 tablespoons minced onion
1 clove garlic, peeled, minced
½ pound cooked ground lamb
(or cooked, ground leftover lamb)
1 cup cooked rice
1 tablespoon chopped parsley
½ teaspoon salt
1 tablespoon minced pine nuts
½ cup fine bread crumbs
½ cup finely grated Parmesan cheese

Wash peppers, cut in half lengthwise and seed. Put enough water to cover peppers in a pan and bring to a boil. Cook peppers in the water for 3 minutes. Drain. Cool. Sauté onion and garlic in oil until golden. Add meat, rice, parsley, salt and pine nuts. Stir and cook for 2 minutes. Stuff the pepper halves with stuffing. Mix the bread crumbs and cheese and top the stuffing with this mixture. Arrange peppers in ½ cup water in a shallow baking pan. Bake at 350° for 25 minutes.

ROYAL GREEN BEANS

4 tablespoons butter
½ onion, peeled, minced
3 tablespoons minced parsley
3 tablespoons flour
½ teaspoon salt
¼ teaspoon pepper
2 tablespoons grated lemon peel
1 cup sour cream
4 cups cooked French-style green beans

Melt butter and sauté onion until golden. Add parsley and flour and stir until flour is slightly cooked. Remove from fire. Add salt, pepper, lemon peel and sour cream and mix well. Add beans and stir until coated with cream mixture. Put into shallow baking dish and bake in 325° oven for 15 minutes. Serves 6.

"Many shops stood in the street, and Dorothy saw that everything in them was green."

SOLDIER WITH GREEN WHISKERS SALAD

Peeled avocados
Green peppers
Seedless green grapes
Zucchini slices
Slivered scallions

Peel avocados and cut in half lengthwise. Discard pits. (Allow ½ avocado for each salad.) Put avocado halves cut-side down on salad plates. Make a soldier face using green pepper strips for his mouth, a large piece of green pepper for his hat, zucchini slices for his spectacles, a green grape for his nose and lots of slivered scallions for his beard.

"The people were all dressed in clothing of a lovely emerald-green color and wore peaked hats."

Braised Pork Chops & Green Cabbage

6 pork chops
1 large onion, peeled, sliced
1 large firm green cabbage, cut into 6 wedges
1 cup beef bouillon

Cut the excess fat off the chops and fry the bits of fat over low heat in heavy casserole until brown. Discard bits. Turn up heat and brown chops. Add onion and fry until translucent. Cover and simmer until chops are tender. Add cabbage and bouillon. Cover and simmer for 5 minutes or more until cabbage is just barely tender. Serves 6.

" 'There is no hope for me,' she said, sadly, 'for Oz will not send me home until I have killed the Wicked Witch of the West; and that I can never do.' Her friends were sorry, but could do nothing to help her; so she went to her own room and lay down on the bed and cried herself to sleep. "

74

GREEN APPLE CRISP

4 large or 6 medium green apples
¼ cup sugar
Pinch of salt
1 tablespoon water
1 tablespoon lemon juice
Sprinkle of nutmeg

Top crust:
½ cup sugar
½ cup flour
½ teaspoon baking powder
2 tablespoons butter
1 egg

Wash, pare, core and slice apples. Put apple slices into a mixing bowl and add sugar, salt, water, lemon juice and nutmeg. Mix well. Put into a buttered 9″ x 9″ pan.

Crust: Mix sugar, flour, baking powder, butter and egg and cream together until of spreading consistency. Dip a spatula into cold water and spread dough evenly over apple slices. Bake at 325° for 45 minutes or until golden brown on top. Serve warm with whipped cream on top.

LIME SHERBET

¾ cup sugar
1¾ cups water
1 tablespoon gelatin dissolved in ¼ cup cold water
½ cup fresh lime juice
Few drops green food coloring
2 egg whites
⅛ teaspoon salt

Put sugar and water into a saucepan and bring to a boil. Boil for 10 minutes. Remove from fire, add gelatin and let cool for 5 minutes. Add lime juice and food coloring. Chill in a freezer tray until mixture begins to solidify. Whip mixture with a wire whisk or fork until fluffy. Beat egg whites until stiff. Add salt and fold egg whites into gelatin mixture. Freeze for 4 hours, stirring thoroughly several times as the sherbet chills.

EMERALD CITY PICNIC CHICKEN

A 3-pound frying chicken, cut into serving pieces
¼ cup flour
½ teaspoon salt
½ teaspoon pepper
¼ teaspoon thyme
¼ cup cooking oil
¼ cup minced parsley

Pat chicken dry with paper towels. Put flour, salt, pepper and thyme in a brown paper bag. Put chicken pieces into the bag, a few at a time, and shake to coat them. Put the cooking oil into an oblong shallow baking pan (8″ x 12″). Roll each chicken piece around in the oil until well coated and arrange in a single layer in the pan. Bake at 375° for 40 minutes or until the chicken pieces are tender and brown. Sprinkle with parsley.

"The green girl was very kind to them, filled Dorothy's basket with good things to eat, and fastened a little bell around Toto's neck with a green ribbon."

Green Ribbon Potato Salad

4 cups boiled, peeled, sliced salad potatoes
½ cup chopped scallions
½ cup chopped celery
⅓ cup chopped radishes
4 hard-cooked, peeled, sliced eggs
Salt and pepper to taste
¾ cup mayonnaise
Sliced green olives for topping

Lightly mix potatoes, scallions, celery, radishes and eggs in a bowl. Add salt and pepper. Add mayonnaise and mix carefully until all ingredients are slightly coated with dressing. Add more mayonnaise if the mixture appears too dry. Put into a serving bowl and top with olive slices.

HILL CLIMBERS' CHICKEN SOUP

2 tablespoons butter
1 medium onion, peeled, minced
1 stalk celery, washed, chopped
2 tablespoons flour
2 teaspoons curry powder
3 cups chicken broth
1 cup half-and-half
1 cup cooked, shredded white chicken meat
Salt and pepper to taste

Melt butter in deep, heavy saucepan. Add onion and celery and cook until vegetables are tender. Stir in flour and curry powder. Add broth slowly, cooking and stirring until well blended and slightly thickened. Add half-and-half and stir well. Add chicken. Simmer for another 5 minutes. Season to taste. Serve hot.

"The Emerald City was soon left far behind. As they advanced the ground became rougher and hillier, for there were no farms nor houses in this country of the yellow Winkies which was ruled over by the Wicked Witch of the West."

COUNTRY OF
THE WINKIES

YELLOW BEAN SALAD

1 pound yellow wax beans
4 slices bacon
½ cup finely minced onion
½ cup vinegar
⅛ teaspoon paprika
1 teaspoon sugar

Nip off ends of beans. Wash, cut French style by slicing lengthwise. Put into saucepan with water to cover. Bring to a boil and then simmer gently until barely tender. Drain and set aside. Sauté bacon until crisp. Remove bacon from pan, reserving fat. Pat bacon with paper towels, cool slightly, then crumble. Add onion, vinegar, paprika and sugar to bacon fat and cook for a couple of minutes. Pour hot dressing over beans and toss. Sprinkle top with crumbled bacon and serve immediately.

BROWN SUGAR MELTAWAYS

3 cups brown sugar
1 cup light cream
¼ teaspoon salt
2 tablespoons butter
1 teaspoon fresh lemon juice

Combine sugar, cream and salt in heavy saucepan. Cook and stir over medium heat until mixture boils, then turn down heat and cook, without stirring, until mixture reaches soft-ball stage (238°). Remove from heat. Add butter. Let mixture cool to 110°. Beat until creamy. Add lemon juice and beat a little more. Drop by teaspoonfuls onto a buttered platter. When cool, wrap individually in foil or waxed paper. Makes a pound of candy.

"'See what you have done!' the Wicked Witch screamed. 'In a minute I shall melt away.' 'I'm very sorry, indeed,' said Dorothy, who was truly frightened to see the Witch actually melting away like brown sugar before her very eyes."

THE WONDERFUL
WINKIE OMELET

3 tablespoons cooking oil or butter
1 medium onion, peeled, chopped
3 medium zucchini, washed, sliced thin
1 cup sliced fresh, washed mushrooms
1 cup chopped fresh, washed spinach leaves
6 eggs, beaten
½ teaspoon salt
¼ teaspoon pepper
1 cup chopped fresh tomatoes
½ cup grated Swiss or Parmesan cheese

Sauté onion in large frying pan or flameproof casserole until translucent. Add zucchini and mushrooms. Sauté for 5 minutes. Add spinach. Cook and stir for 5 minutes. Turn out into shallow baking dish. Beat eggs. Add salt and pepper and pour over vegetables. Put tomatoes on top. Sprinkle with cheese. Bake uncovered at 350° for 20 minutes or until eggs are set.

"The Winkies rescued the Tin Woodman and carried him back to the castle where their tinsmiths worked for three days and four nights mending him so that he was as good as new."

YELLOW COUNTRY SEAFOOD CASSEROLE

2 cups string beans, sliced lengthwise
½ cup olive oil
1 teaspoon paprika
2 onions, peeled, sliced vertically
2 pimentos, sliced
1 pound fish filets (any firm, white fish such as haddock)
1½ cups rice
2 tablespoons butter and oil for sautéing rice
1 clove garlic, peeled, minced
2 teaspoons salt
½ teaspoon oregano
¼ teaspoon pepper
¼ teaspoon saffron
½ cup chopped parsley
3 cups chicken broth
1 dozen shrimp or prawns, shelled, de-veined

Boil string beans in water to cover until tender. Drain and set aside. Add paprika to olive oil and put into frying pan. Heat until hot, then add onions and sauté until golden. Add pimentos. Bone fish and cut into 2-inch cubes. Wash rice in cold water thoroughly and drain. Heat butter and oil in frying pan and sauté until grains are coated with oil. Put all ingredients into heavy Dutch oven and stir well. Cover and bake in 325° oven for 45 minutes. Serves 6.

FREEDOM DAY LEMON CHICKEN

A 3-pound frying chicken, cut into serving pieces
Salt and pepper to taste
3 tablespoons butter
3 tablespoons minced green onions
3 tablespoons minced fresh parsley
⅓ cup fresh lemon juice
Lemon slices for garnish

Sprinkle the chicken with salt and pepper. Melt butter in heavy frying pan and sauté chicken pieces until brown, turning on all sides for browning evenly. Add onions, parsley and lemon juice. Cover and cook over low heat for about 20 minutes, or until chicken is tender. Remove to serving dish and garnish with lemon slices.

"Dorothy's first act was to call the Winkies together and tell them they were no longer slaves of the Wicked Witch. There was great rejoicing among them and they kept this day as a holiday, and spent the time in feasting and dancing."

WINGED MONKEY MACAROONS

¼ pound shredded coconut
1 teaspoon vanilla extract
⅛ teaspoon salt
Sweetened condensed milk
2 egg whites

Combine coconut, vanilla, salt and enough condensed milk to make a thick batter. Beat egg whites until stiff and fold in. Drop batter from a teaspoon onto a greased cookie sheet keeping mounds of batter about 1½ inches apart. Bake at 250° about 30 minutes or until golden.

"On the way to the Emerald City, the King of the Winged Monkeys told Dorothy the story of the beautiful princess Gayelette and her husband Quelala, the first owner of the charmed Golden Cap."

QUELALA'S WILD RICE CASSEROLE

A 4 – 6-pound roasting chicken, cut into serving pieces
1 pound pork sausage
1 pound mushrooms, cleaned, sliced
1½ cups sliced onions
2 cups wild rice
¼ cup flour mixed with ½ cup light cream
2½ cups chicken broth
1 teaspoon rosemary, crushed
½ teaspoon thyme, crushed
1 teaspon salt
½ teaspoon pepper

Prepare the wild rice:
2 cups wild rice
8 cups cold water
½ teaspoon salt

Combine rice and water and bring slowly to a boil. Boil for 5 minutes. Remove from heat and drain. Repeat this process 3 times, skimming hulls that float to the top of the water each time. If kernels are not expanded and fluffy, repeat the process a fourth time. Add the salt to the last water.

Remove skin from chicken pieces. Poach chicken in water

to cover until barely tender. Sauté sausage until brown, remove meat and set aside. Sauté mushrooms and onions in sausage fat until onions are translucent. Put rice, mushrooms, onions and crumbled sausage into a bowl and mix. Add flour and cream mixture to the broth and stir until blended. Pour over rice mixture. Add seasonings and mix. Put a layer of the rice mixture in a large casserole, lay chicken pieces on top and add the rest of the rice mixture. Bake covered in 350° oven for 30 minutes. Serves 6.

WINGED MONKEY BANANA SAUTÉ

Firm, ripe bananas (allow 1 banana per serving)
Butter
Brown sugar
Lemon juice

Peel and slice bananas in half lengthwise. Heat a tablespoon of butter in a frying pan until the butter bubbles. Fry banana slices until golden brown on both sides. Transfer to serving dishes and sprinkle bananas with brown sugar and lemon juice.

Humbug
Chicken Legs

8 10-inch skewers
1 pound veal steak, cut into 1½-inch cubes
1 pound pork steak, cut into 1½-inch cubes
½ teaspoon salt
½ teaspoon pepper
½ cup flour
1 egg, mixed with 3 tablespoons water
1 cup bread crumbs
¼ cup cooking oil
2 tablespoons minced onion
1½ cups chicken stock, made with 2 bouillon cubes and
2 cups boiling water

Put veal and pork cubes on skewers, alternating veal and pork. Press together to shape like a drumstick. Mix salt, pepper and flour together and put on a shallow plate. Put egg and water mixture in a shallow dish. Put bread crumbs in a shallow dish. Heat oil in large frying pan until hot. Roll skewered meat first in seasoned flour, then in egg mixture, then in crumbs. Brown meat on all sides. Transfer to Dutch oven. Sauté onion until translucent, and add to meat. Pour stock over meat. Cover and bake at 325° for 50 to 60 minutes until meat is tender.

"'Exactly so!' declared the little man, rubbing his hands together as if it pleased him. 'I am a humbug.'"

FOOL-THE-EYE CHERRY PIE

1½ cups cranberries, washed, cut in halves
¾ cup sugar
1 tablespoon flour
1 teaspoon almond extract
1 teaspoon butter

Pastry for 2 (9-inch) crusts:
2 cups flour
⅓ teaspoon salt
⅔ cup shortening
4 to 6 tablespoons ice water

Put flour, salt and shortening into a mixing bowl and blend with your fingertips until the mixture is the consistency of corn meal. Add ice water a tablespoon at a time, while tossing mixture with a fork, until a soft dough is formed. Divide dough in half. Roll out between two sheets of waxed paper until large enough to fit a 9-inch pie pan.

Line a pie pan with crust. Fill crust with cranberries. Mix sugar and flour and sprinkle over cranberries. Add extract. Dot with butter. Cover with top crust. Bake at 425° for 10 minutes, then at 400° for 30 minutes or more until crust is lightly browned.

THE WIZARD'S GIANT PRETZELS

1 cake compressed yeast or 1 package dry yeast
1½ cups warm water
1 tablespoon sugar
1 teaspoon salt
4 cups flour
Cornmeal
1 egg, beaten
Coarse salt

Dissolve yeast in warm water in large mixing bowl. Add sugar and salt and stir well. Add flour, one cup at a time, beating after each addition. Turn dough out onto a floured board and knead until smooth. Cut off small chunks of the dough, roll into half-inch-thick ropes and twist into pretzel shapes. Dust cookie sheets with corn meal, arrange pretzels on the sheets, brush tops of pretzels with beaten egg, and sprinkle generously with salt. Bake in a hot oven at 425° for 15 minutes or until brown. Makes 6 or 8 large pretzels.

"'I have fooled everyone so long that I thought I should never be found out,' said the Wizard."

SUPERIOR BRAN MUFFINS

1 cup sifted flour
2 teaspoons baking powder
½ teaspoon soda
½ teaspoon salt
1½ cups 100% bran cereal
¼ cup raisins
¼ cup chopped nuts
⅓ cup butter
¼ cup brown sugar
1 egg, beaten
1 cup buttermilk

Sift flour, baking powder, soda and salt together in a large mixing bowl. Add bran, raisins and nuts and mix. Cream butter and sugar together until light. Add egg and blend into creamed mixture. Add creamed mixture and buttermilk alternately to dry mixture, stirring until mixed. The batter should be slightly lumpy. Fill greased muffin tins ⅔ full. Bake at 400° for 20 minutes or until golden. Serve hot. Makes 1 dozen.

"'Hereafter you will be a great man, for I have given you a lot of bran new brains,' said the Wizard to the Scarecrow."

KIND HEART CAKES

1¾ cups sifted cake flour
2 teaspoons baking powder
¼ teaspoon salt
⅔ cup butter
1 teaspoon vanilla
1 cup sugar
2 eggs, well beaten
½ cup milk
1½ dozen red candy hearts or cinnamon drops

Sift flour, baking powder and salt together into a mixing bowl and set aside. In another bowl, cream butter and sugar together until light and fluffy. Add vanilla and blend. Combine eggs and milk and add to creamed mixture alternately with sifted ingredients, beating after each addition until smooth. Line muffin tins with paper baking cups or grease muffin tin cups. Fill each about ½ full of batter. Put a red candy heart in each one, then add batter until cups are each ⅔ full. Bake at 350° for 15 to 20 minutes.

"Then, going to a chest of drawers, the Wizard took out a pretty heart, made entirely of silk and stuffed with sawdust. 'Isn't it a beauty?' he asked. 'It is indeed!' replied the Woodman, 'but is it a kind heart?' 'Oh, very!' answered Oz."

LIQUID COURAGE

4 oz. grape juice
1 tablespoon sugar
Juice of ½ lime
4 oz. soda water

Combine grape juice, sugar and lime juice in a pitcher and stir well. Pour into an 8-oz. glass. Add soda water. Serve over crushed ice.

"The Lion hesitated no longer, but drank till the dish was empty. 'How do you feel now?' asked Oz. 'Full of courage,' replied the Lion."

CHINA PRINCESS PECAN BRITTLE

1½ cups light brown sugar
¼ cup light corn syrup
¼ teaspoon cream of tartar
¼ cup water
1 cup broken pecan meats
2 tablespoons butter
1 teaspoon soda

Put sugar, syrup, cream of tartar and water into deep, heavy saucepan and boil until candy thermometer registers 250° (hard-ball stage). Add pecans and boil until thermometer registers 300° (hard-crack stage). Add butter, remove from heat, add soda and stir vigorously. Pour onto buttered platter and spread thin. When cold, cut or break into pieces.

"Before them was a great stretch of country having a floor as smooth and shining and white as the bottom of a big platter. Scattered around were many houses made entirely of china and painted in the brightest colors."

CHINA COW MILK SHAKE

2 scoops vanilla ice cream
1 cup cold milk

Put ice cream and milk into a blender. Blend until ingredients are thoroughly blended. Pour into a tall glass.

"They began walking through the country of the china people and the first thing they came to was a china milk-maid milking a china cow. As they drew near, the cow suddenly gave a kick and kicked over the stool, the pail, and even the milk-maid herself."

MR. JOKER'S STICK CANDY

1¼ cups sugar
¼ cup water
2 tablespoons corn syrup
2 tablespoons white vinegar
1½ teaspoons butter
½ teaspoon vanilla

Put sugar, water, syrup, vinegar and butter into small, deep, heavy saucepan and bring mixture to a boil stirring until the sugar is dissolved. Cook over medium heat, without stirring, until candy thermometer registers 270° (soft-crack stage). Remove from heat and add vanilla. Stir thoroughly. Pour out carefully onto a buttered platter (10″ to 12″ diameter). Let the candy cool for a few minutes. **Do not touch it until it is cool enough to handle.** Butter your fingertips and pick up the mass of candy and pull it, stretching it about a foot in distance between your hands each time you pull. Pull it until it becomes light in color and quite stiff. Roll it into a ½-inch-thick rope. Cut into 3″ lengths and wrap each stick in waxed paper.

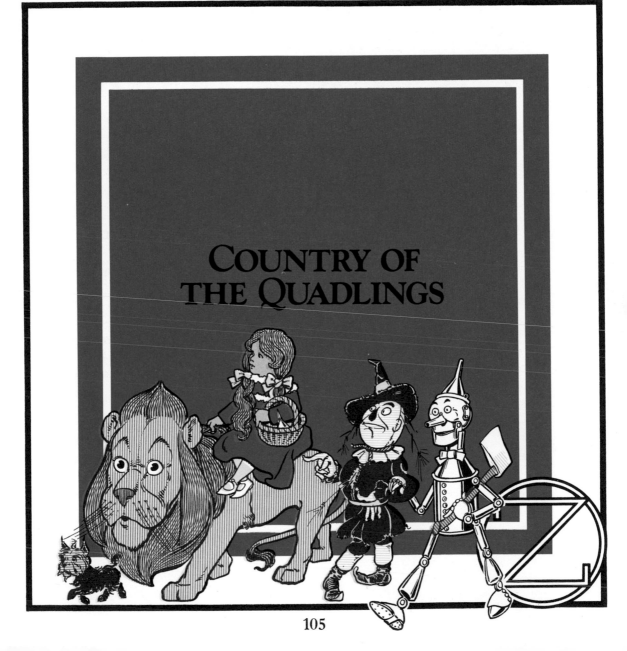

COUNTRY OF
THE QUADLINGS

HOT TOMATO SOUP

1 quart fresh, ripe tomatoes, peeled, chopped
Pinch of soda
1 cup water
1 teaspoon sugar
1 medium onion, peeled, chopped
2 tablespoons butter or margarine
Parsley for garnish

Cream Sauce:
2 tablespoons butter or margarine
2 tablespoons flour
1 teaspoon salt
½ teaspoon pepper
1 quart milk or half-and-half

Prepare tomatoes by dropping them first into boiling water for a couple of minutes, then into cold water. Peel, chop. Put tomatoes into a soup pot with the soda and water and simmer until tender. Add sugar. Sauté onion in butter until translucent and set aside.

Make the cream sauce: Melt butter, stir in flour, then add salt and pepper. Pour milk slowly into butter mixture, stirring constantly, and bring to a boil. Add to tomatoes. Add onions. Stir well. Sprinkle with parsley and serve.

COLD TOMATO SOUP

6 medium tomatoes, peeled, minced
1 onion, peeled, minced
1 (4-oz.) can pimentos, drained, minced
1 medium cucumber, peeled, seeded, minced
1 clove garlic, peeled, minced
¼ cup olive oil
3 teaspoons vinegar
4 teaspoons salt
¼ teaspoon pepper
⅛ teaspoon cayenne pepper
1½ cups tomato juice

Garnish:
Small bowls of chopped scallions, celery,
ripe olives, and parsley

Put all of the ingredients into a large bowl. Stir well. Cover
and refrigerate until very cold. When you serve the soup,
put one ice cube in each bowl and pass the small bowls of
scallions, celery, olives and parsley for garnish.

"The country of the Quadlings seemed rich and happy.
The fences and bridges and houses were all painted bright
red. The Quadlings themselves, who were short and fat and
looked chubby and good-natured, were dressed all in red."

BAKED STUFFED RED SNAPPER

A 4 – 5-pound whole red snapper, cleaned, rubbed with salt inside

Stuffing:
¼ cup chopped onions
¼ cup butter
4 cups soft bread crumbs
Juice of ½ lemon
2 teaspoons salt
1½ teaspoons poultry seasoning
1 teaspoon freshly ground black pepper
3 tablespoons chopped parsley

Brown the onions in butter in a heavy frying pan. Mix with crumbs, lemon juice, salt, pepper, poultry seasoning and parsley. Stuff the fish, then sew or fasten sides together with skewers. Rub the outside of the fish with cooking oil. Put in oiled roasting pan. Bake at 400° for 10 minutes a pound for fish weighing up to 4 pounds. Add 5 minutes per pound to the total baking time for each additional pound. When the fish is tender and brown, remove thread or skewers and serve with stuffing.

QUADLING BURGERS

2 pounds good quality ground beef
1 medium onion, peeled, chopped
1 green pepper, seeded, chopped
1 cup celery, chopped
2 tablespoons brown sugar
1 tablespoon red wine vinegar
1 tablespoon A-1 sauce
2 tablespoons Worcestershire sauce
1 tablespoon prepared mustard
½ cup catsup
1 can tomato soup
1 dozen hamburger buns

Put oil in heavy stew pot. Brown beef. Add onions and brown. Add rest of ingredients. Simmer, covered, for ½ hour. Serve hot in hamburger buns.

RED CASTLE HOT DOGS

Wieners (2 per person)
Cheese strips
Bacon slices

Cut a lengthwise slit in each wiener. Cut a strip of cheese ¼-inch thick the same length as the slit. Fill the slit with the strip of cheese, wrap a slice of bacon around each stuffed wiener and fasten ends with toothpicks. Broil wieners slowly, turning often, until the bacon and wieners are cooked through and brown.

"When they were all quite presentable they followed the soldier girl into a big room where the Good Witch Glinda sat upon a throne of rubies."

RED COUNTRY SPAGHETTI SAUCE

6 tablespoons olive oil
6 tablespoons butter
5 cloves garlic, peeled, minced
2 onions, peeled, chopped
1 pound each: ground veal, ground pork, ground beef
2 carrots, scraped, grated
3 whole cloves
2 stalks celery, washed, chopped
1 teaspoon ground thyme
1 teaspoon dried basil
2 large cans (28-oz.) tomatoes
2 cups beef bouillon
Salt and pepper to taste
1 small can (6-oz.) tomato paste
Parmesan cheese for garnish

Heat oil and butter in heavy, deep pot. Add onions and garlic and sauté until golden. Add ground meat, crumbling the meat as you add it to the pot. Chop, cook and stir until meat is browned. Add all the rest of the ingredients, except tomato paste, and stir until thoroughly mixed. Simmer for 3 hours, covered. Add tomato paste and cook uncovered for another 15 minutes. Serve with hot, freshly-cooked thin spaghetti and sprinkle with fine-ground Parmesan cheese. (This sauce can be frozen for later use.)

Golden Cap Salad

(4 individual salads)
1 package (3-oz.) lemon gelatin
1 cup boiling water
½ cup cold water
1 tablespoon multicolored cake décors
4 rings of canned pineapple
4 maraschino cherries

Put gelatin in a bowl. Add boiling water and stir until gelatin is dissolved. Add cold water and stir well. Butter 4 custard cups. Sprinkle a few décors into each cup. Put equal amounts of gelatin in cups and chill until gelatin is firm. *To unmold:* Set cups in a pan of hot water for about 10 seconds. Put a pie plate on top of cup and holding plate tight to cup, invert cup and shake mold out. Put a ring of pineapple on a lettuce leaf on a salad plate. Put gelatin mold on top and top the mold with a cherry.

"'Bless your dear heart,' Glinda said, 'I am sure I can tell you of a way to get back to Kansas. But, if I do, you must give me the Golden Cap.'"

RASPBERRY CREAM CAKE

1½ cups cake flour, sifted before measuring
2 teaspoons baking powder
¼ teaspoon salt
1 cup sugar
½ cup butter
¾ cup milk
1 teaspoon vanilla
3 egg whites
2 cups fresh raspberries for topping and filling

Sift flour, baking powder and salt together and set aside. Cream sugar and butter together until light and fluffy. Combine milk and vanilla and add to creamed mixture, stirring until blended. Add sifted mixture to creamed mixture about half a cupful at a time, stirring well after each addition. Beat egg whites until stiff and fold into the batter carefully. Grease 2 9-inch round cake tins and put half of the batter into each one of them. Bake at 375° for 25 minutes or until a toothpick inserted in the center of the layers comes out clean. Cool on a rack. Remove from pans.

Whipped cream frosting:
3 tablespoons powdered sugar
1⅓ cups heavy cream
½ teaspoon vanilla

Sift the sugar and set aside. Beat the cream until it stands in peaks and is stiff. Add sugar and fold into cream. Add vanilla and blend. Spread the top of 1 layer with whipped cream

mixture and top with 1 cupful of raspberries. Add top layer. Make a layer of the rest of the raspberries. Frost top and sides with the rest of the cream mixture.

THREE-STEP CHOCOLATE SUNDAE

Scoops of vanilla ice cream

Sauce:
1 cup powdered sugar
1 egg
¼ teaspoon salt
2 squares unsweetened chocolate
2 tablespoons butter
Cream to thin

1. Put sugar, egg, salt and chocolate in heavy saucepan over low heat and stir and cook until chocolate is dissolved. DO NOT BOIL.
2. Remove from heat, add butter and stir well.
3. Thin with a few tablespoons of cream to desired consistency. Serve immediately over scoops of ice cream.

"The Silver Shoes have wonderful powers. They can carry you to any place in the world in three steps."

HOME AGAIN

AUNT EM'S CABBAGE SALAD

¼ cup vinegar
1 tablespoon sugar
½ teaspoon salt
¼ teaspoon pepper
½ teaspoon dry mustard
1 tablespoon butter
1 egg, beaten
2 tablespoons cream
3 cups finely shredded cabbage

Put vinegar, sugar, salt, pepper, mustard and butter into a saucepan and heat to the boiling point. Add a few table-spoonfuls of hot mixture to beaten egg, then stir egg mixture into hot mixture and cook and stir until mixture thickens and boils. Remove from heat. Add cream and beat. Pour over cabbage and stir well. Chill. Serve cold.

" 'My darling child,' cried Aunt Em, 'where in the world did you come from?'

" 'From the Land of Oz,' said Dorothy gravely, 'and oh, Aunt Em, I'm so glad to be at home again!' "

HOME AGAIN POT ROAST

4 pounds beef chuck
2 tablespoons flour
1 teaspoon salt
½ teaspoon pepper
⅛ pound salt pork, with rind removed
1½ cups hot water
1 bay leaf
Few sprigs of parsley
8 small white onions, peeled
4 large carrots, scraped, cut into chunks
8 small potatoes

Sprinkle meat with flour, salt and pepper. Fry salt pork over medium heat in heavy stew pot to generate fat to brown the meat in. Brown meat on all sides. Add hot water, bay leaf and parsley. Cover and simmer for about 3 hours, adding a little water if needed to keep bottom of pan covered with water. During the last hour of cooking, add onions and carrots. During last half-hour of cooking, add potatoes.

To thicken the drippings for gravy: Pour off drippings into frying pan. Add 1 cup water. Mix 2 tablespoons of cornstarch with ¼ cup cold water and stir until cornstarch is dissolved. Add to hot drippings, stirring constantly until mixture thickens.

WATERMELON PICKLES

2 pounds watermelon rind, peeled, soaked in salted water
1 tablespoon cinnamon
1 teaspoon whole cloves
1 teaspoon whole allspice
2 pounds sugar
1 pint vinegar
1 pint water
1 lemon, sliced thin

Peel inside pink flesh and outside green skin from rind and cut into 2″ pieces. Soak rind overnight in salted water, using ¼ cup salt to each quart of water. Drain off salt water, put into deep pot, add clear water to cover and cook until tender. Drain, set aside rind and boil the rest of the ingredients in the pot for 5 minutes, stirring until sugar dissolves. Add drained rind to this pickling solution and boil over high heat until rind becomes translucent. Cool. Remove spices from syrup with slotted spoon. Pack pickles in clean glass jars, cover with pickling solution and store in refrigerator.

120

STRAWBERRY SHORTCAKE

1 quart fresh strawberries

Wash, hull and cut in half, leaving a few whole for topping. Add ½ cup of sugar or more depending on how sweet you like them. Mix and let stand.

Biscuits:
2 cups flour
4 teaspoons baking powder
1 tablespoon sugar
½ teaspoon salt
⅓ cup butter
1 egg, beaten
¾ cup milk
Whipped cream for topping

Sift dry ingredients. Add butter and mix lightly with finger-tips until mixture resembles coarse meal. Mix egg and milk and add. Stir until soft dough is formed. Drop by table-spoonfuls onto greased cookie sheet. Makes 8 biscuits. Bake at 375° for 15 minutes or until golden. Split biscuits and fill with berries. Put a couple tablespoonfuls of whipped cream on top of each biscuit and top with a few whole berries.

COOKING TERMS

Bake: To cook in the oven.

Baste: To spoon liquid over food as it cooks.

Batter: A mixture of flour and liquid that is thin enough to pour or drop from a spoon.

Beat: To mix vigorously with a spoon, whisk, or rotary beater. **Note:** To make stiff egg whites, beat until they are frothy and light enough to stand in peaks when the beater or whisk is lifted up.

Blend: To mix gently until ingredients are combined.

Boil: To cook over heat until bubbling.

Brown: To cook, usually with a small amount of oil over high heat, until brown.

Chop: To cut into small pieces with a knife.

Cream: To beat with a rotary beater until mixture is soft and creamy. If a beater isn't handy, the mixture can be creamed by rubbing the ingredients against the side of a mixing bowl with the back of a heavy spoon. **Note:** When creaming butter, the process is less work if the butter is at room temperature before you begin.

Cube: To cut into small, square pieces.

Dissolve: To stir an ingredient into liquid until absorbed. **Note:** When dissolving yeast, take care that the dissolving liquid is lukewarm, not hot. Hot liquid will kill the yeast and the bread will not rise.

Dough: A thick mixture of flour, liquid and other ingredients.

Drain: To pour off liquid from food that has been soaked or cooked, or to put fried food on absorbent paper.

Dutch Oven: A heavy iron pot with a tight-fitting lid.

Flake: To separate into thin layers, using a fork.

Fold: To combine ingredients gently by turning them over and over in a bowl using an in-and-out motion with a spoon or rubber spatula.

Fry: To cook in hot oil or fat over high heat.

Grate: To shred into very small pieces by rubbing the food against a grater.

Grease: To swab the bottom of a frying pan or the inside of a baking dish with cooking oil or shortening to prevent food from sticking.

Hard-ball Stage: 250°F. If you don't have a candy thermometer, drop a small amount of the candy mixture into a small dish of cold water. When a hard mass is formed, mixture is at the hard-ball stage.

Hard-crack Stage: 300°F. If you don't have a candy thermometer, drop a small amount of the candy mixture into a small dish of cold water. When mixture leaves threads when leaving the spoon and a brittle mass is formed, mixture is at the hard-crack stage.

Knead: A repeated flattening and folding movement made with the heels of the hands. See directions for Munchkin Currant Bread, page 30.

Lukewarm: Comfortably warm, not hot.

Melt: To cook over low heat until a solid, usually butter or chocolate, becomes liquid.

Meringue: A mixture of egg white and sugar, beaten stiff.

Mince: To cut or chop into very small pieces.

Mix: To stir until all ingredients are combined.

Poach: To cook gently in simmering liquid.

Preheat: To heat pan or oven before putting food into it.

Sauté: To fry lightly in a shallow pan with oil, butter, or margarine.

Scald: To bring almost to the boiling point.

Sear: To brown the outside of a piece of meat quickly over high heat before reducing heat to cook at a more moderate rate.

Seed: To remove seeds from fruits or vegetables.

Separate: To divide the white from the yolk of an egg. First, crack the eggshell, holding together both halves of the shell. Then, gently pull them apart and tip the yolk into one half of the shell. Let the white run into a bowl. Put the yolk into a separate bowl.

Shortening: Fats, usually butter, vegetable oils, or margarine, used in cooking.

Sift: To put flour or other ingredients through a sifter or wire mesh sieve.

Simmer: To cook gently in liquid, without boiling.

Skim: To remove fat or matter that forms on top of a liquid, usually after it has been boiled.

Soft-ball Stage: 238°F. If you don't have a candy thermometer, drop a small amount of the hot candy mixture into a small dish of cold water. When a soft mass is formed, mixture is at the soft-ball stage.

Soft-crack Stage: 270°F. If you don't have a candy thermometer, drop a small amount of the mixture into a small dish of cold water. When the mixture separates into hard threads, it is at the soft-crack stage.

Soften: To let butter or margarine stand at room temperature until soft.

Tender: To cook until food can be easily penetrated with a cooking fork.

Translucent: To cook until food is partially transparent.

INDEX

PICKLES
Watermelon Pickles   120

PIES
Fool-the-Eye Cherry Pie   94
Green Apple Crisp   75

PUDDINGS
Imperial Rice Pudding   58
Magic Lemon Pudding   27
Upside-Down Pudding   18

SALADS
Aunt Em's Cabbage Salad   118
Cowardly Lion
    Quivering Gelatin   52
Golden Cap Salad   112
Green Ribbon
    Potato Salad   78
Soldier with Green
    Whiskers Salad   72
Spinach Salad   69
Yellow Bean Salad   82

SANDWICHES
Bacon and Cheese Bricks   39
Haystack Sandwiches   44
Hot Cheese Sandwiches   56
Peanut Butter Toast   43
Red Onion and
    Bacon Sandwiches   39
Scarecrow Sandwiches   44

SNACKS
Field Mouse Nibbles   55
Gatekeeper's Cheese Log   67
Scarecrow Survival Snacks   43
Tin Woodman Chips   48
Tin Woodman
    Nuts & Bolts   50

SOUPS
Cold Tomato Soup   107
Green Split Pea Soup   68
Hill Climbers'
    Chicken Soup   79
Hot Tomato Soup   106

VEGETABLES
Quick & Easy Corn Sauté   40
Royal Green Beans   71
Stuffed Green Peppers   70